THEATRE ETIQUETTE UNMASKED!

MARGARETTE JOYNER

Published by Pecan Tree Publishing
Dania, FL

Theatre Etiquette Unmasked
Margarette Joyner

Pecan Tree Publishing
Dania Beach, FL
www.pecantreebooks.com

Library of Congress Catalog Card Number: On File

979-8-9938089-2-5 Paperback
979-8-9938089-3-2 Ebook

Book Design Concept by E. Claudette Freeman
Cover and Interior Design by Charlyne Strachan
Interior images licensed through Envato Cover images licensed through IStock

This book is dedicated to all the "Old School" theatre practitioners who blessed me with their wisdom.

PREFACE

As a singer, I have come to appreciate how powerful and moving performance art can be. I recognized this at a young age, but I didn't fully grasp its significance until my voice grew stronger. I knew when I sang, people would close their eyes, shake their heads, raise their hands, and say, "Sang child, sang." This let me know my singing was good, but I didn't quite comprehend why they reacted like that. The enlightenment came when I understood the uniqueness of the gift I'd been given and the realization that there was no other voice like mine. I came across this realization when I drowned out the years of noise from folks who told me I was too loud. I learned to manage it by being loud when I needed it and soft when I didn't. By honing my voice in this manner, I was able to study my own voice and understood that the richness and sincerity of it actually eased pain. That's when I realized the power behind the chords.

As an actress, my performances have brought audience members to tears, and it was not because I was great, but because the storytelling touched them in a very personal way. I wrote and performed a one-woman show which spoke about my journey from being raised by a mother who didn't know how to show love, to me looking for love in the wrong places. I didn't just tell the story; I relived it in front of audiences without any inhibitions. Women would approach me after the shows, unable to speak or only having the words, "You just told my story." The story gave them a sense of comfort knowing they weren't alone. That's when I realized the power of storytelling.

My specialty in designing and constructing costumes is based on being mindful and considerate of "fluffy" performers. They are performers, according to society, who are considered large because they are bigger than a size twelve. I worked at a regional theatre for twelve years and that was my gift. Ironically, they started calling me "the heavy hitter" because I could construct specified clothing that others in the shop could not. As one reviewer put it, "Margarette Joyner's costumes are simply amazing. The finery she puts her actors in is breathtaking and looks like every nickel of her budget ended up on stage." I realized how crucial this was when an actress came in for a fitting wearing anxiety. It was our first meeting, and when our eyes connected, I could tell she needed something. I asked her if she was okay. She replied no and explained how she had always allowed others to make her feel bad about herself because of her size. Tragically, this would happen during fittings. I reassured her that she would not have that experience that day. I then asked the designer, cutter/draper and first hand to please step out of the room until I got her dressed in her first look. I put her in her first dress without chiding her but instead complimenting her on how beautiful she was and how much I loved her voice. This put her at ease. When I turned her around to look in the full-length mirror she gasped and expressed how elegant she looked. Dress after dress made her more and more emotional as she saw the couture garments I put together for her. By the end of the fitting, she was in tears and told me she had never felt more beautiful than she did that day. That's when I realized the power clothing could have on a person.

As artists, we must all recognize that what we do may not cure anything, but it certainly does heal.

FOREWORD

In my role as an educator and practitioner of theatre, I am observing that in this age of technology, widespread trepidation and instant gratification, a vital part of theatre has been lost. What's lost? Etiquette! It saddens me to see young people, in particular, struggling with social skills. They find it difficult to communicate without the use of a cell phone or they have challenges with overwhelming anxieties that are literally debilitating them. Seasoned practitioners, like Gen X and Baby Boomers, accuse the younger generation of not having thick enough skin, being lazy, lacking ambition or being heavily reliant on medication. While some, or all of these things may be true, I'm also of the belief that they didn't turn out this way fully due to their own fruition. The biggest culprit, I believe, was COVID! We were all stuck inside with little to do and whatever we did was through technology.

For approximately two years theatre students and practitioners were without a stage, with limited instruction, and with little communication on a human level. Then, upon return to face-to-face interactions, another culprit came into play. They were pacified and coddled to such an extent that they found it difficult to cope with the slightest amount of "real" work. The real work of being able to give their all without fear of how they may look in front of their peers or an audience became a challenge. Taking the effort to do the research and put in the time necessary to develop a character and embrace the whole story has become overwhelming. From what I have witnessed, and although it has been several years since the height of COVID, the transition is still ongoing. It has become traumatizing for educators, designers and directors who are having to do far more than teach. Nowadays, we are required to adhere to numerous accommodation letters for students, recognize the artists who are medicated for mental challenges, and be mindful of triggering words, actions, and certain plays. *("We don't want to do trauma plays; we just want to have fun!")* While we are taking care of students and artists, the question remains: "Who is taking care of us?" We went through COVID too. Not to mention, some of us are struggling to keep up with the fast pace of technology!

As an educator and director, my mission with this book is to enlighten some and remind others of the ins and outs of theatre etiquette. Etiquette the way it used to be taught. When we signed a contract, it meant our word was binding. I trust it will also remind directors, designers, stage managers, and other theatre practitioners of what should be expected in the space. Also, to reiterate that the chain of command is a real thing. The Producers come first because they are the ones paying the bills, and then realizing the Director's vision is the goal! My hope is that it will also assist in bringing a higher level of respect back to the theatre, fostering better communication, and creating an atmosphere of joy on the journey.

The time for pacification must end so that we can get back to truth-telling in all aspects of theatre and film without fear. I hope a newfound perspective will eliminate negative energy from a lack of understanding and bring back the "play" in play. This book is raw and therefore not for the faint of heart. But if you are interested in growth and becoming the theatre person that everyone will want to work with, brace yourself, take it all in and then put it into practice.

CONTENTS

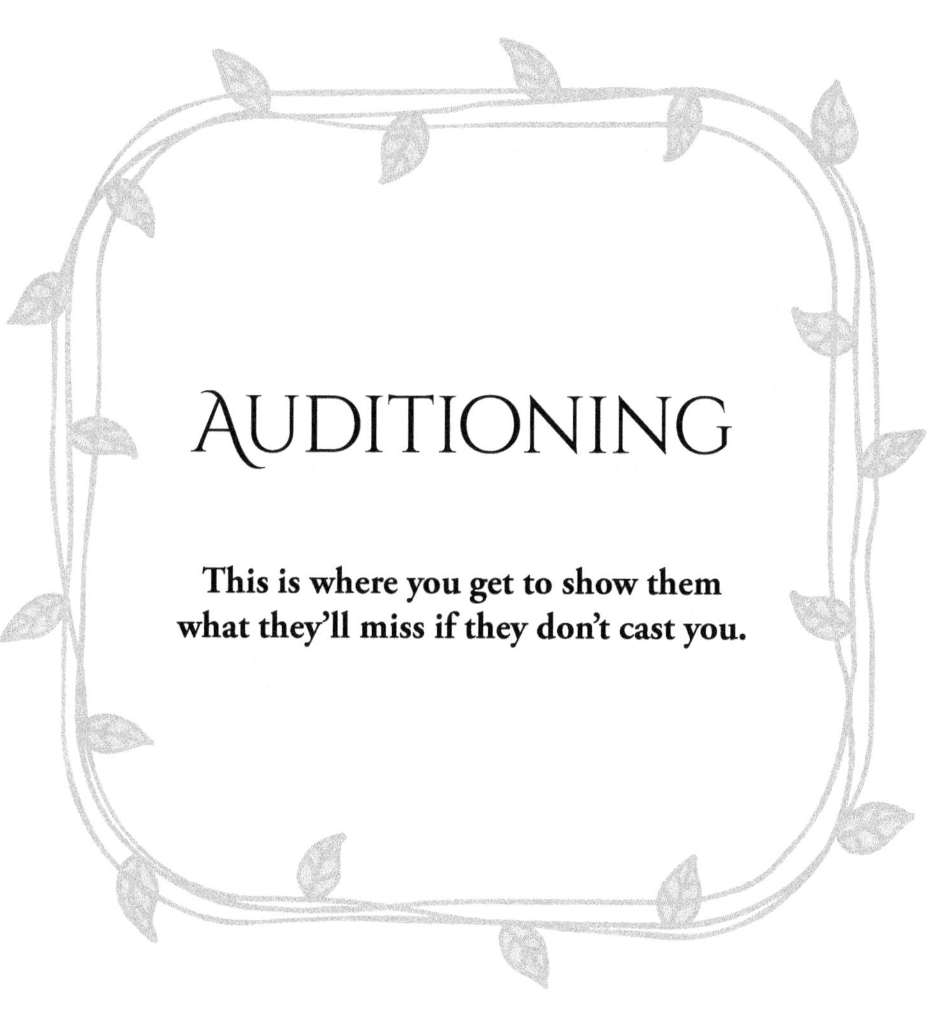

AUDITIONING

This is where you get to show them what they'll miss if they don't cast you.

When I decided to pursue a theatre degree, I was well into my forties and already considered myself a seasoned performer. While this was true, I also realized that my lack of formal training was limiting me. I had what's called "raw talent." Acting came naturally to me, but when a director told me to go upstage left, I didn't know what that meant, and they had to explain it. For this reason, I went to school, learned all things theatre, and during that time earned several awards. These included a scholarship to **Dad's Garage** in Atlanta and placing fourth out of some 600 performers at the Kennedy Center American College Theatre Festival. As an undergraduate, that was quite a feat! I earned a Bachelor of Fine Arts from the University of South Alabama and headed up to New York right away. New York was the place everyone said I needed to be. I was that good and, to top it off, I had a voice that could fill a room without a microphone! Luckily, a friend of mine had an apartment in Harlem and was on his way to direct a show in Miami. He gave me his apartment at no charge for six months while he was gone. I packed up all my things, got in my little gold pickup truck *(Goldie)*, and headed to New York.

After getting over being traumatized by the bigness of EVERYTHING, I landed a job in a costume shop because of my sewing skills. What a miserable experience that was! The owner had a cat and told me that if it jumped up on the table while I was cutting, I simply needed to cut around it. Needless to say, I lasted about three weeks before I quit. I got another job in a shop where the owner screamed at everyone on a daily basis for the slightest mistake. Once, he screamed at me, for what felt like an hour straight for cutting the wrong thing. Then, he made me stand at the ironing table pressing fabric for six hours. That was one of several days that I cried on the job because I wanted to quit but needed the money. Later that week, he screamed at me again, only to realize I cut exactly what he had written on the pattern. Did he apologize? Of course not. Instead, he wanted to know, Why are there dishes in the sink when there's a room full of women in the shop?" But I digress.

After a month or so of finding my balance, I went to my first audition. When I walked into the building where the audition was being held, I was stunned by the number of aspiring actors, dancers, and singers present. I saw dancers stretching on legs that were taller than me, actors doing their lip trills at a speed I'd never seen before, and singers "me, me, me-ing" with fierce intensity. As I walked through the crowd, I could feel the eyes on my four-foot-long dreadlocks. I heard whispers and a few giggles as I passed by and I immediately felt small, less than and intimidated, but I stayed. I found a little spot in a corner and sat there going over my monologue and song for hours. When I was finally called into the room, no one at the table looked up at me. I was terrified! Nonetheless, I nervously gave my sheet music to the pianist and then presented an introduction. Next, I performed my monologue, giving it everything that I had. No one looked up, but I persevered. I nodded to the accompanist and what he played was unrecognizable. Regardless, I tried to sing anyway and was completely off key. I thought I would sink into the floor. He stopped, and asked, "What key do you want?" I had no idea; I hadn't studied music. I looked at him, and I knew he saw how lost I was. He called me over to the piano and after a brief collaboration, he knew what to do. He started the song again and this time it was in my key and on my tempo. By the time I'd gotten to the climax of the sixteen bars, everyone at the table had eyes on me. The belting voice I had developed reverberated around the room, out the windows and throughout the halls. I got the callback! When I walked out of the room, the crowd that had looked down on me now applauded. It was the most frightening and the best audition I'd had. Although I didn't get cast in that show because I wasn't a dancer, I did get cast in another. The key here is that no matter what the circumstances look like or feel like, there is only one you and, if you give it everything you've got, you'll stand out and be remembered.

Tips for Auditioning

1. Before you audition, do your research and familiarize yourself with the play, the characters, the playwright, and who you're auditioning for. If you know something about the company, the director will be impressed and you'll be able to honestly explain why you want the part and why you want to work with the company. It will also help you to be better prepared to answer any questions asked about your monologue.

2. When you get to the audition, do not engage with other auditioners unless they invite you to do so. They are often in a 'zone' and may not want to be disturbed, so don't take it personally.

3. The audition process typically involves the following steps:

   a. Check in and wait to be called.
   b. You may be asked to deliver your prepared monologue, perform a song, or cold read.
   c. You may also be asked to perform a scene with others.

4. In the case of cold readings, where you are reading parts from the script with little or no time to prepare, take your time to go over the material thoroughly after you receive it and before going in to audition.

5. Whenever possible, practice your prepared monologue in front of someone who will give you an honest critique.

6. Make sure you get a good night's sleep the night before your audition and have a bite to eat before you go. You don't want to have a full meal as it can make you feel tired, but eat enough so that your stomach doesn't growl during the performance.

7. The audition is a performance, so give it your all and enjoy it!

8. Invest in a good character shoe. These can be used in dance auditions as well as character auditions as they are supportive and classy.

9. If you are singing, stay away from chocolate and dairy because it makes your mouth water. Tea with honey is ideal.

10. Always warm up before your audition. This is particularly important because it releases tension you may not even know you are carrying. Your warm up should include some breathing exercises, stretches for loosening up the body and vocal exercises.

    Recommended Breathing Techniques

    Diaphragmatic Breathing: Focus on deep breathing using your diaphragm rather than shallow chest breathing. This helps enhance relaxation and reduce stress.

    Box Breathing: Inhale for a count of four, hold for four, exhale for four, and hold again for four. Repeat this cycle to effectively calm your mind.

    Calming Breathing Technique: Inhale through the nostrils for a count of four into the belly, exhale out the mouth for a count of four. This technique can be done anywhere and is beneficial for stress and anxiety. Regular practice enhances its effectiveness.

    Alternate Nostril Breathing: This technique involves breathing through one nostril at a time, which can help balance the nervous system and improve emotional regulation.

11. Put your phone away while awaiting your turn so that your character is easily accessible after your introduction. If you are distracted by looking at something else on your phone just before you go in, that is where your mind will be instead of getting into character. It will take you several precious seconds

to get fully into character and directors will be able to tell if your head and heart are truly in it. You will leave the audition knowing you didn't give it your all.

12. Beware of sabotaging yourself with fear of rejection or not getting the role.

13. Do not be distracted by comparing yourself to anyone else. Self-confidence is your lifeline, not arrogance, but genuine self-confidence.

    When I went to auditions, and saw that a certain actress was there, I would immediately tell myself that I was not going to get cast. Most of the time, I didn't . The truth is, it wasn't always because she gave a better read, but because I allowed intimidation to defeat me before I even entered the room.

    Remember, you are just as good as anyone else. You might not have gotten cast because your hair was too long or too short, or they were looking for a specific sound or even because the part called for someone with a peg leg! You never know the real reason, so do your best and keep it moving!

Once, I auditioned for a movie that I knew, without a doubt, I would get. I made it all the way to the final callback, only to receive the dreadful 'they went in a different direction' call from my agent. When I saw the movie, I was baffled because, no shade, but really? Then my agent told me, "They wanted to cast you, but she had a bigger name."

14. Be kind and respectful to the person with the clipboard. *(the assistant to the assistant to the assistant's assistant, you get the picture).* They may seem unimportant, but they stand between you and the audition panel. They set the tone for you before you walk through the door, and their opinion matters to the folks behind the table.

15. Walk in with intention, a hello, and a smile.

16. If you are asked about feeling nervous, always tell them that you are excited to be there.

17. Do not apologize for any mishaps. It is okay to ask to start over, they want you to succeed and will not hold that against you. Instead, most will admire your willingness to own your mistake and your bravery in pushing through.

18. If you have a scene partner who is not what you need them to be, you be all *you* need to be without making them look bad.

19. Only offer a handshake if they offer it first. They might be a germaphobe *(a person with an extreme fear of germs and an obsession with cleanliness)*, so having them reject you could throw you off balance.

20. Understand that your audition begins the moment you walk through the door or get out of your seat, not when you get on stage. Your body language informs the director whether you are prepared or not, and instantly communicates whether you are confident or arrogant and hungry or desperate. To be absolutely clear, you want to convey preparation, confidence, and hunger.

21. Wear clothing that is complementary to your body, comfortable to move in and modest. Black is your friend! Directors don't

want to see your chest spilling over your shirt or your pants sagging. If you show up looking like you just got out of bed or are coming from the gym, they won't take you seriously. You should have several black 'theatre outfits' specifically for auditioning. Aim for loose-fitting bottoms and a fitted top if your body type allows it; otherwise, stick to loose-fitting *(but not sloppy)* tops and bottoms. You're a professional, so dress accordingly.

22. Know exactly what happened in the script right before your monologue begins. If your character starts off upset, you must know why they are upset and with whom. Allow your physicality to speak before you utter your first word. This crucial context only comes from reading the whole script.

23. During your introduction, keep it real! Be yourself. They want to get a peek into who you are, the real you and they'll know instantly if you are just 'acting' real.

24. Please have your monologue memorized. Do NOT read your monologue from your phone, no matter what anyone says! It is unprofessional and shows that you did not think enough of the job to prepare for it. Who told you that was okay? It is definitely **NOT** okay!

25. Make sure you have a minimum of two contrasting monologues ready. When you are asked to present a second monologue, the director or casting agent is looking to see what your range is. Let them have it and show no fear of being free or looking crazy!

26. Present pieces that you perform well consistently. They may ask you to repeat your monologue, but this time, do it in a different scenario, such as while you're exercising. If you are solid on your monologue, this won't throw you off balance.

    There was a time when an actor auditioned for me, and I could tell they were 'acting,' but when I asked them to pull up a chair and give their monologue to my assistant as if they were speaking with a friend, they blew it out of the water. It was raw, it was real, and it got them cast! In another case, I asked an auditioner to repeat their monologue while pretending to be drunk in order for me to see how comfortable they were in their body. They attempted it but couldn't do it because their inhibitions got in the way. They were not cast. This test told me that I would have little to work with in that actor. I didn't want to work that hard!

27. Please time your pieces; it shows you know how to follow directions. A one-minute monologue should be about 45 seconds, a two-minute monologue should be about one minute and 45 seconds and a three-minute monologue should be about two minutes and 45 seconds. This buffer gives you some wiggle room for beats *(pauses)*.

28. Avoid profanity, political and spiritual views in your audition. At all costs, avoid monologues that belittle or mock a specific type of person *(for example, homophobic, racist, damnable content)*. Understandably, we live in a world of shock culture, but it's not always appropriate in this professional setting, so play it safe.

    I had someone audition for me using a monologue where the character was physically and mentally challenged. It was so real, but it made me uncomfortable because I didn't know how to feel after the monologue ended. I also didn't know how to cast her, since the piece was so unorthodox and outside the realm of the play I was casting. My assistant lamented, "Somebody needs to tell her not to ever do that again." I asked her why she felt that way and she explained that she has a brother who is autistic and unless that's the specific role I was looking for, it shouldn't be the kind of material one uses.

29. The audition and the monologue should genuinely mean something to you! You should be able to answer the questions instantly: Why is it important to you? What's at stake? And why did you choose this specific monologue?

30. Always have a strong choice piece. Old school performers used to call this a 'money piece.' This is the monologue you know like the back of your hand, which almost always ensures you're heard and gets you hired.

31. Self-written pieces should only be used as a last resort. Without published material, there's nothing for the director to compare your interpretation to, which makes it impossible for them to know if you've 'done it right.'

32. DO NOT present monologues from movies or audition books. They've heard them all!! **READ PLAYS!!** You should continually read plays of all kinds; you never know when a monologue will jump out at you that you can genuinely connect with. Directors will sit up and take notice of the people who bring them something from a play they haven't heard before.

33. Don't do anything you can't give 100% to. A piece that's 'easy' but done well is much better than something 'hard' done badly.

34. Always know the name of the play and the author of your piece. This information should be part of your introduction. The playwright deserves the recognition, and providing it shows your respect for their work.

35. If you perform a popular piece, make sure you present it with an interpretation that is entirely unique to you. Remember: just because countless others have performed it one way doesn't mean you have to follow suit.

36. Be aware of your breath. If you feel like you're running out of air before the end of your sentence, it's okay to take a breath to ensure you are heard. Trailing off at the end of sentences causes the listener to wonder what you said. Consequently, they may miss the next sentence because they're still trying to figure out the previous one.

37. Understand that each audition is unique and there are no absolutes. There is always more than one way to do a thing. So, if someone says, "I've always heard it done this way," ignore them and do what feels right to you. It doesn't mean your way is better; it's just different.

38. Do not make eye contact with the director or casting agent when presenting your monologue. This forces them to be a part of the performance against their will and makes them uncomfortable. If you observe them looking down or writing, seemingly not paying attention, it's because they choose not to participate in your presentation. Instead, pick a spot above their heads if you're talking full frontal, or place your invisible scene partner in an empty chair. If you're talking to no one in particular, remember what it feels like when you're by yourself and expressing how you truly feel: you may close your eyes, pace the floor, look up, look down, or look all around. Do the same in the audition.

39. Professional theatre actors always have at least six monologues they can draw from: two dramatic, two comedic and two classics *(e.g., Tragedies from ancient Greece, Roman comedies, Shakespearean).*

40. Auditioning for parts that are not specifically written for you is a great idea. If a company is producing a play that has a cast they envision one way, your audition could make them see the role in an entirely different light. Furthermore, approaching diverse material will help you explore your range and give you valuable practice.

41. For music auditions, make sure the accompanist knows exactly what you need. Your music sheet should be clearly marked with 'start here' and 'end here' to ensure a smooth transition.

42. Make sure your music sheet is backed by something *(like card-stock or a binder)* that allows it to stand up easily on the piano's music rest. This simple step ensures that if a door opens and a breeze passes through, your music won't fly off the piano.

43. Make sure you know the exact key you need the accompanist to play and be ready to state it clearly.

44. Always have a range of songs that you know well, including: one up-tempo, one ballad, one classical, one gospel/spiritual, one folk and of course, a musical theatre piece.

45. Directors usually ask for 16 or 32 bars. Give them exactly what they ask for and nothing more. If you exceed the request, they will likely cut you off and note that you do not know how to follow directions.

46. Never, ever try a new piece for the first time on the day of the audition. Your audition pieces need to be polished and excep-

tionally well-rehearsed so that even if the accompanist gets the music wrong, you can plow past it and keep going.

47. Don't bother with props, unnecessary activities, or gimmicks. ACT! The focus should always be on your performance, not your visual aids.

48. Impromptu skills, the ability to respond without preparation and think on your feet, will teach you to work quickly. Instant script or environment changes offer the opportunity to use those skills, which is especially important for films where script revisions happen frequently. Taking an improv class or workshop will definitely help with this. In the meantime, here is a link to some improv games. Remember, when you're not in a show, you should be studying.

    https://teambuilding.com/blog/improv-games

49. Auditions will open doors for you even if you don't get cast. Casting agents and directors will remember you if you are impressive. They may not be able to use you in the specific production you auditioned for, but they will certainly keep you in mind for future projects.

50. Think about auditioning as a dedicated platform where you have the chance to act, sing, or dance in front of a captive audience that is there just for you!

51. Qualities of a good audition:

    a. Concentration - Act as if nothing else is in the room.
    b. Truth - Be authentically you!
    c. Spontaneity - Take it one moment at a time.
    d. Specificity - Make choices specific to the scene or character.
    e. Energy - Be creative and energetic, even if it's a quiet energy.
    f. Humor - Know where the humor is and play without pushing. Never "go for" the laugh; it usually falls flat.
    g. Courage - Commit to your choices; have no fear.
    h. Skill - You've got this!

52. When you are called back after an audition, have a different monologue or song ready to show the director how much range you have.

I'm sharing all of these tips with you so that you will give your absolute all at every audition and get cast consistently.

REHEARSALS

Rehearsals are a place for discoveries and for you to put into practice "the work" you've been doing outside of scheduled rehearsals. This includes consistently applying the notes you received at the previous rehearsal.

I wrote a play titled **"Sweet Chocolate and the Seven Christians."** I allowed a young practitioner to direct it to give her some experience. She was excellent, but was struggling to earn the respect of the young cast, as most of the actors were her peers.

Normally, I don't attend rehearsals when someone is directing one of my plays because I prefer to give them room to explore without anyone being intimidated by my presence. However, as the show's producer, I responded immediately when she asked me to observe a rehearsal. I arrived about fifteen minutes before rehearsal started and knew immediately that I needed to have a 'Come to Jesus' meeting with them.

The cast members who were present were on their phones, listening to music through earbuds, eating full-course meals or engrossed in deep conversations about relationships, while others strolled in nonchalantly. At seven-fifteen when almost everyone had arrived, I got the cast's attention and began giving them instructions on what they should be doing as an ensemble. A few minutes into the speech, an actor walked in the door carrying a large plastic cup with a long straw inserted. As she made her way to take a seat, she stumbled and fell into one of the audience seats, which she found quite funny.

I tried to begin again, but noticed that her attention was clearly not on anything in the room, especially me. Her eyes were glazed over, and as the room grew quieter, I observed her until our eyes finally connected. I could immediately tell something was not right. I'd seen that look many times before. You know, the one where someone is looking right at you but doesn't actually see you.

I asked, "Are you drunk?"

She wobbled her head and slurred, "I've had a few drinks, but I wouldn't say I'm drunk."

I was momentarily speechless, and a complete hush fell over the room because, although the cast had not been in an ensemble state of mind, they all knew better than to show up intoxicated. They also knew me and waited with bated breath to see how I would respond. *(I had garnered a reputation for firing actors who thought they could get away with coming up short, especially close to opening night. Not on my watch!)*

I asked, "Are you drinking right now?"

She replied, "Yeah, but I'm almost finished," as she took another slurp of her beverage.

I smiled to keep from biting her head off and told her she needed to leave. She said okay without question and stood up to make her exit. She stumbled down the stairs, mumbling something about not knowing why I was 'tripping' just because she was 'a little tipsy.' Her final protest was, "I can still rehearse."

It took everything I had in me not to laugh at the sheer audacity and ridiculousness of the situation, especially since some of the cast members were struggling to contain themselves. Instead of being upset, I allowed them to release that tension and laughter by asking, "What in the ham sandwich was that? Are you kidding me? I'm almost finished! Doesn't she know that if she finishes the drink, she's only going to get drunker?"

The entire room erupted, and I joined them. Once we gathered our composure, I completed my spiel, and the director didn't have any more problems after that. The moral of this story is: if you are not going to take the job you've been given seriously, find something else to do.

Make Rehearsals Magic

1. The rehearsal process usually begins with a 'table read' of the play, where the cast literally sits at a table and reads the script aloud so everyone can hear the words come to life. Afterward, a discussion typically focuses on the play's overall themes. Actors share their research and the director outlines their overall vision. Be sure to have read the play and have something to bring to the table, even if it's only questions.

2. Come to rehearsal **prepared to work**! No one really cares what kind of day you had, they probably had a horrible one too. Rehearsal is where you get to shake off the real world and play in someone else's. Embrace that fact and enjoy the process!

3. Please do not come to rehearsal with a poor attitude. No one in the room caused whatever is upsetting you, so making your colleagues endure your wrath is not fair. Negativity spreads like a disease and can destroy the entire atmosphere of the space. Leave it at the door!

4. Make sure you warm up your voice before you arrive at rehearsal. You can do lip trills, vocal exercises, or tongue twisters to prepare. Here are a few of my favorites:

    a. Brisk brave brigadiers brandished broad bright blades, blunderbusses, and bludgeons - balancing them badly.
    b. If a black bug bleeds black blood, what color blood does a blue bug bleed?
    c. How many cookies could a good cook cook if a good cook could cook cookies? A good cook could cook as many cookies as a good cook who could cook cookies.
    d. Which wristwatches are Swiss wristwatches?
    e. I wish to wish the wish you wish to wish, but if you wish the wish the witch wishes, I won't wish the wish you wish to wish.

Try saying each one three times if you can!

Also, think about reading them with an accent, conveying different emotions, or using various registers *(high and low)* of your voice. Have fun with them!

5. Wear comfortable, closed-toe shoes to work in. Flip flops, high heels, slides, and Crocs are unacceptable unless the footwear is explicitly character-related. If that is the case, bring them with you to change into after warmups. Safety is key.

6. Fifteen minutes before rehearsal starts is considered being on time. For example, if rehearsal is scheduled for 7:00, you should be warmed up, on stage and ready to go at 7:00 sharp. In case you missed it: if you walk in the door at 7:00, you're late!

7. If you are going to be late, it is your responsibility to inform the Stage Manager as soon as possible. The best way to do this is to text them. Never call another cast member or the director; they are on time and working, so do not disturb them. When you arrive, quietly put your belongings down and immediately get

into your respective area. The director or stage manager should not have to ask you to join in simply because you walked in, took a seat, and waited to be told what to do.

8. If you need to eat because you didn't get dinner between work and rehearsal, either eat on your way to rehearsal or bring finger foods/snacks that you can eat during your 10- or 15-minute break. Let me repeat that: only eat during your 10- or 15-minute break, not while your character is off stage.

9. Always bring a <u>**pencil**</u> to rehearsals for writing down notes and blocking given by the director. **A <u>pencil</u>** is essential because it allows you to easily erase and adjust staging, as the director's vision may evolve from one day to the next. It is your job to write notes in your script so that you can incorporate them while studying for the next rehearsal. Trust me, you won't remember everything once you leave. How many times have you heard a director say, "I gave you that note before."

10. When the director gives you a note, the correct response is simply "Thank you." Unless you don't understand the note, in which case the response is "Please clarify." No other commentary is necessary, it wastes valuable time. Even if you don't agree with the note, try it anyway. If it doesn't feel right, bring the director an alternative choice at the next rehearsal and ask if you can share it. If they don't like the new choice, your job is to make their direction work. Remember, you can't see what the director sees, and the overall vision belongs to them. Also, no professional director will intentionally have you looking bad on stage; if you look bad, they look bad. So, trust them.

11. What the director told you to do yesterday doesn't matter; do what they tell you to do TODAY! *(That's why you have a pencil and eraser).*

I was in a rehearsal when an actor made the fatal mistake of reminding the director of yesterday's direction after receiving a new directive. The director bluntly replied, "I don't give a **** what I told you to do yesterday; you do what the **** I told you to do, today!" The actor complied and had nothing further to say.

12. If you thought you were already doing what the director gave you a note on, it means the performance of the intended action didn't translate to them. Take the note and try something different.

13. When the director is working with other actors, use that time to focus on your lines, characterization, and feedback while you wait. This is **NOT** the time for you to be on your phone.

14. When official breaks are called, put your script down and take the time to step away. Allowing your mind to rest will help you recharge and rejuvenate for the next scene.

15. Actors **DO NOT** give other actors notes. For the people in the back, **ACTORS DO NOT GIVE OTHER ACTORS NOTES!!** That responsibility belongs exclusively to the Director and Stage Manager. The energy you spend focusing on someone else's performance is better channeled toward your own development. Mind your own business!

    Quite some time ago I was cast in a show alongside a rival actor. We often found ourselves in the same audition room; sometimes I'd get the role, sometimes she would. In this particular production, however, we were both cast, but I got the lead role. Throughout the rehearsal process she repeatedly tried to give me notes, which initially annoyed me. Then, I decided to ignore her, eventually allowing the situation to escalate to the point where I would deliberately do the total opposite of what she suggested. *(I know, petty, but that's who I was at the time).* She would be so frustrated with me, that I soon discovered that laughing at her and dismissing her instructions eventually turned her frustration into outright anger. It brought me joy. *(Again, petty).* One evening as we drew closer to opening night, the director gave me the very same note she had been offering. Before the director could finish his note, she shot to her feet and announced, “I’ve been trying to tell her that for days!” What happened after that is a blur: my anger surged so quickly that, before either of us fully registered what was happening we were literally at each other’s throats ready to fight. Of course, the Stage Management and other actors intervened immediately to prevent the fight. However, the remainder of rehearsal and the run of the show was intense to say the least. While certainly not my proudest moment, the point remains: Mind your own business!!

16. If you have any issues during the process, the proper protocol is to talk to your Stage Manager first. Do not approach other actors, the director, designers, or technicians. The Stage Manager is the ‘gatekeeper’ and must be your first point of contact.

17. Do your homework! Figure out what your character was doing before the play started. Analyze their character, know what their relationship is with the other characters in the story.

18. DO NOT stop rehearsal unless it is a safety issue! The only individuals authorized to halt a rehearsal are the Director or the Stage Manager.

19. Learn your lines!! Get off-book well before the deadline. A director can take your performance to heights you didn’t know you could reach, but not until you **LEARN YOUR LINES!!!!**

20. Look at a script as if it were a mountain you have to climb. The only way to conquer it is one hill at a time.

21. Tech rehearsals are tedious, time-consuming, and long. Maintain patience, be kind and remember that this necessary process is only to ensure that you look good on stage.

If you follow these points, you will become what's known as a "director's actor." This means you will become an actor that a director will want to collaborate with repeatedly. I can attest that once you achieve this status, directors will often reach out to you and request your participation in their show without auditioning.

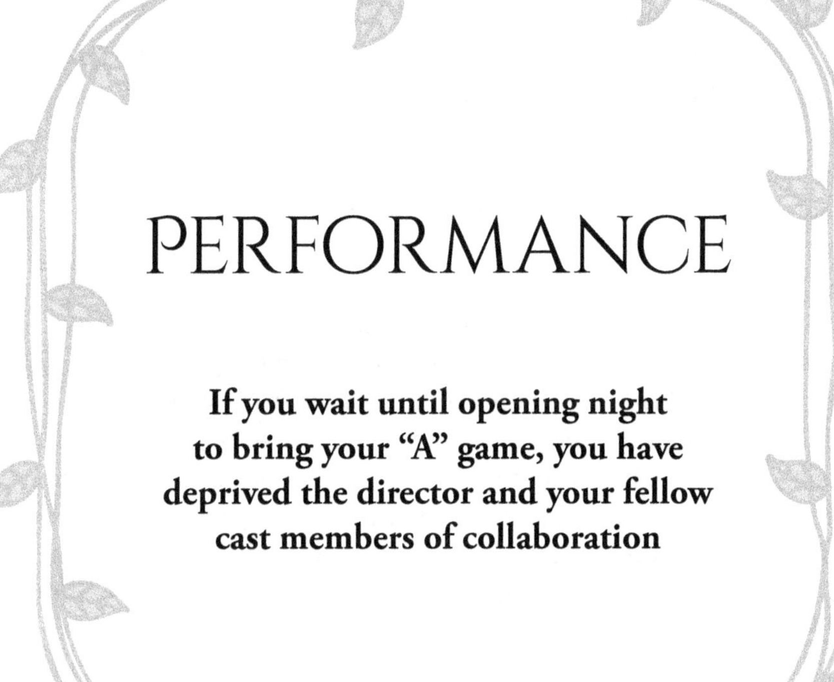

PERFORMANCE

If you wait until opening night to bring your "A" game, you have deprived the director and your fellow cast members of collaboration

Once a show has been directed and opened, it then belongs to the Stage Manager and the cast. However, that does not grant them permission to jeopardize the integrity of the director's vision or the playwright's words. I directed a show that, if I do say so myself, was intensely lovely. Opening night was well-received and left some audience members in tears. The accolades the cast and I received were enough to boost anyone's ego and were humbly welcomed by all. I felt good enough about the production that I went on to another project, causing me to miss several performances. When I returned to see the final performance, I was shocked to see that one of the actors had changed some of the blocking, dismissed some of the props, was delivering lines differently, and had removed some lines altogether. Needless to say, I was insulted and extremely disappointed. But more than that, I was deeply hurt because I trusted them with our work. The message that cast member sent by making all those decisions without consulting me was clear: they felt they could direct the show better than me with my three decades of experience, while they still had milk around their mouth! *(Just a baby in the industry)*. What they didn't understand is that I based my direction on the overall vision and what was best for the entire production, and not on just their performance. This type of behavior is how directors realize they will never work with you again, and will certainly share that information with their colleagues. The performance community is small; everyone knows everyone, or at least they **know** someone who does. So, always be respectful.

Performing with Pride

1. Your presence on stage is solely to serve: Serve the story, serve the ensemble, and serve the audience. It's not about you!

2. The first step to becoming a great performer is the ability to be open. To be open, you must be honest and willing to be vulnerable in front of strangers.

3. Be someone whom others will welcome working with. Divas are not cute! Your attitude can get you blackballed quickly. I will work with an inexperienced talent who has a willingness to learn rather than an experienced actor who thinks the curtain rises and falls on them.

4. Keep your body in shape to do what you love. This doesn't mean you must be a certain size; it means you should have enough stamina to carry you through the run of a show. On Broadway, for instance, that means eight shows per week.

5. Water should be your best friend. It will keep you hydrated, prevent your throat from being dry and is key to a healthy body.

6. **CHECK YOUR PROPS!!!** Yes, the Stage Manager handles this, but they are human and capable of making mistakes just as we all are. It is your job to double-check and ensure you have everything needed to have a successful performance.

7. Understand the difference between intense and loud. There is a huge difference! Loud is all about volume, whereas intensity is about power, which is not always loud. Think of it this way. If you're watching an actor and they are flailing their arms, crying, and screaming at their scene partner, while the other actor on the receiving end has deadly eyes, clenched jaws, fists tight and measured breathing while responding quietly, the question is, who is more powerful? This distinction is crucial, especially in film, where the camera is so close it can almost see your nostril hairs. You must know the difference.

The first time I went to a film audition, they knew immediately that I was a theatre actor because of how loud I was. It was there that I learned the difference. My audition was great, but they had to tell me to pull it back and taught me how to "read the room." In other words, I had to learn how to adjust my big voice as it pertained to the space I was in. Big room? Blow the roof off! A small room? Fill it with quiet intensity.

8. Every performance is different but you must always be in the moment. On opening night, the adrenaline is high and the excitement of seeing that first audience is exhilarating! That energy pushes you to limits you didn't even know you had. That exact level should be applied to every show, whether it's a full house or an audience of one. Every performance is opening night!

9. Be present even when you're not speaking. You can easily get distracted if you are not paying attention to what's happening in the given circumstances. The key is to always be listening. This will also prepare you in case someone gets lost. Be the "catcher" on stage, and your ensemble will appreciate you. If someone drops a line or gets lost in the story, you will be so familiar with everyone's lines and the story that you will be able to "catch" them when they fall.

10. Knowing the story is a must! If you "go up" on a line *(miss it)*, you can recover if you know where you are in the story. Otherwise, you may jump entire scenes without realizing it.

Knowing the story will also allow you to assist your fellow cast-mates if they get stuck or lost.

11. If you are not feeling the emotion you need on stage, do not fake it. If you can't cry, then don't force it, because someone like me will see right through a false emotion.

12. When performing for children, talk to them, not down to or at them. They are much smarter than you think.

13. Always give 100%! Even when you don't feel well or are tired, sad, or anxious, push through and give it everything you've got! The writer and the audience deserve it. After all, they paid to see you!

14. Whispering backstage during a performance is sometimes louder than actually talking. So be quiet!

15. Never be on your phone between scenes during a show. Doing so instantly removes you from the story's environment and deprives the audience of your character's presence during the time it takes to fully get back into character.

16. Contrary to what many performers believe, the bow at the end of the show is not to receive accolades for your performance; it is for you to thank the audience for their presence. They could

have chosen to go anywhere else but instead chose to see your performance. Be grateful.

17. The difference between a good actor and a great one is this: a good actor will tell a compelling story; a great actor will live that story in front of an audience.

18. Once you become fearless, performing and life becomes limitless!

If you have any inhibitions that might deter you from being fully present in the given circumstances of the play, work on it! Otherwise, you could easily fall into the "surface, one-note actor" category and be typecast for the rest of your career. Surface acting is acting from the head and not from the heart. A one note actor means you can only play one type of character, usually without depth. I used to ask actors: When are you going to stop 'acting like' and actually become your character?

TECHIES

You have the most thankless job in the business, yet you are just as important as anyone else. You are the backbone of a production. Without you, the actors would be on stage with nothing and in the dark! I know this because I'm one too. I salute you!

For those who may not be familiar, Techies *(Technicians)* are personnel who are not in the spotlight but who ensure the entire show runs smoothly. They are:

Stage Manager - They are the coordinators of the entire production.

Lighting - Operating lighting boards, setting up spotlights, and creating the desired visual atmosphere.

Sound - Managing microphones, sound consoles, and audio effects to ensure clear sound and music.

Scenery *(or Set Crew)* - Building, painting, and physically moving set pieces on and off the stage.

Costumes - Designing, making, and assembling the clothing, hair and makeup worn by the actors.

Prop Master - Managing the small items *(props)* used by actors or placed on the set.

Run Crew - Working during the performance to manage scene changes, move props, quick change costumes, and operate technical equipment.

I was in a children's show called **"Eager Beaver Builds a Dam"** *by Eugene Jackson*, and during one performance just before intermission, the lights did not fade out when they were supposed to. For a few seconds, which seemed like hours, we didn't know what to do. The lead character started ad-libbing *(making up lines)* to find a way to get us off stage. After a couple of minutes, she found the words to say, and as an ensemble, we followed her lead and made our way off stage. We later found out that the stage manager had fallen asleep in the booth. Needless to say, they were fired on the spot! This goes back to the advice about taking care of yourself. You cannot party half the night away when you have a matinee the next day. You are simply too important to the production to do that!

Can't Tech Without You

1. I realize play productions may be just "skits in the woods" so to speak, but take your job seriously; many people are depending on you. Some say we are not curing anything, and while that may be true, what we are doing is telling great stories and we never know who we may be reaching.

2. When presenting your portfolio to directors or producers to get work, make sure you dress for the occasion. Business casual with a flair of artistry is great!

3. Your portfolio speaks to what you are capable of so make sure it is neat, creative, and professional. It serves as evidence of your past work.

4. Digital portfolios are great and so are physical ones. If you only have a digital copy of your portfolio and the power goes out or your computer is having self-esteem issues, having a physical portfolio will save you. Even if it's a partial binder with your best work, at least you'll have something to present, and it will demonstrate your efficiency to the viewer.

5. Please do not have anything handwritten in your portfolio. It makes it look unpolished.

6. All techies should be at the theatre before the actors. You will need time to set up and have a few moments to exhale before rehearsal starts or the show begins.

7. You should be wearing your black theatre clothing on the first day of tech through the close of the show. Your shoes should be all black, including the soles.

8. If your hair is brightly colored, I would strongly suggest investing in a black skull cap or hoodie so that your presence during scene changes is not distracting. The idea of all black is to make yourself as invisible as possible so as not to pull audience members out of the given circumstances of the play.

9. If your hair is long, pull it back into a bun. You do not want your hair getting caught in any of the moving pieces on stage. This is a serious safety issue!

10. Please do not engage in gossip with anyone about anyone else in the production. Always present yourself as the professional in the room. Find a way to politely let them know that you are concentrating on the show, so "let's have that conversation at another time."

11. The same rules that apply to performers backstage during the show apply to you too. No phone, no talking. You must be fully invested in the show because you never know what might happen.

12. When it is time for scene changes, be the run crew that is known for its timeliness and precision. Move quickly and efficiently around the stage, as dead space in a production can destroy it.

Audience members sitting in the dark for too long makes them antsy and pulls them out of the world of the play.

While working as the Costume Shop Supervisor at **"The Lost Colony,"** a member of the run crew came running in and announced that one of the main characters could not get his zipper to work on his doublet. I asked where he was and they said another runner was bringing him in, but he only had 5 minutes before his entrance.

I announced to my crew that I was going to bark out some orders and not to take it personally, just do what I asked. I asked the run crew person what color the actor's doublet was, and they said silver. I told one stitcher to go thread the industrial sewing machine with gray thread. I told another to grab a seam ripper and another to get me a 15-inch, gray jacket zipper and yet another to thread two hand needles with gray thread.

The actor came into the shop panicked and I tried for about 10 seconds to see if I could get the zipper to work, all the while reassuring him that everything would be okay. I couldn't get it to work, so I took the jacket off him and had his crew members take him to the kitchen area, get him some water, and keep him calm. I threw the jacket on the cutting table and had the person with the seam ripper literally rip the zipper from one side. As she finished that side and began working on the other, I pinned the new zipper onto the finished side. I then ran to the industrial with the stitcher in tow. While I sewed one side, she finished ripping out the old zipper and a third stitcher stepped in to pin the second side with the new one. Within one minute, it was in. I ran back to the cutting table and had two people with hand needles to tack down the ends of the zipper. I called the actor over, slipped him back into his jacket and it closed like butter. The run crew got him back to his place in time for his entrance with thirty seconds to spare. Again, you never know what will happen during a performance and you must be ready at all times and in order to be ready, you must be present.

13. Be the positive light in the room. It'll make for a wonderful experience for everyone involved.

14. If you work on a show and are having a horrible time, *(it can happen)* do the job as best you can by controlling what you can and letting the rest go. Get the paycheck!

15. Once the show opens, the Stage Manager is your go-to person. They have all the elements of the show in their prompt book. If you have questions, concerns, curiosities, or criticisms, go only to your Stage Manager. Do not go to other cast members, the director, the designers, or the producers. Go to the Stage Manager!

As artists, we have a habit of underselling ourselves, especially when we first start out. But remember: you train people how to treat you. You are a skilled artisan and deserve to be treated with respect and to be compensated for the work you do. Yes, you want to build your resume, but working for free is not a habit you should establish. Set a time limit on how long you will work for free, and then commit to the fact that you will not do it anymore. Hence, having a "bill paying" job allows you to set that standard for yourself and turn down jobs that demand more than they're willing to give.

COSTUMES

Performers, first and foremost, show up! And if you don't/can't make your fitting, have the courtesy to call. The unwritten rule is that when you miss your fitting, you must bring chocolate to the shop at your rescheduled visit!

As a costume designer, the first thing I do is read the script in one sitting to gain a complete understanding of the story. Then I wait a couple of days and read the script again, highlighting and taking notes on everything that pertains to what will be worn. This information is mainly indicated in the stage directions and character descriptions, but one can also glean insight from the characters dialogue. For instance, in the play **"The Slumber Party"** *by Emily Claudette Freeman*, several of the characters talk about having been the "fruit loop girls" in high school. They discuss the handmade T-shirts they wore and one of the characters pulls this exact shirt out, surprising the rest of the group.

After reading the script a third time to ensure I've not missed anything, I create a rough costume plot, which is a spreadsheet that tracks what a character is wearing and when they are wearing it. The plot contains no specifics, just items like 'shirt,' 'dress pants,' and so on. Next, I meet with the director to discuss their vision and ensure that what I envisioned while reading the script coincides with what they saw. Once we are on the same page, I am free to let my creativity flow by researching time periods, pulling pictures for my inspiration board, and creating sketches. After that, there are design meetings with other designers *(Set, Lighting, etc.)* to make sure all of our designs are in conversation with one another. If my costume color choice is in contrast with the set color, we have to address that. Once everyone has collaborated, achieved a unified vision, and received the director's final approval, the realization of the costumes begins. This phase involves meeting with the costume shop, shopping, organizing, attending fittings, and making garments. This process demonstrates the amount of work that goes into costume designing, so please be sure to respect those who are trained to do it. At the designer's presentation to the cast, I deliver this warning: If they have something negative to say about my costumes, they open the door for me, as an experienced director, to comment on their acting! That usually does the trick!

Costume Consideration

1. Performers, once you accept the role, you are not to change anything about your appearance without checking in with the designer! No haircuts, no hair coloring, and no crash diets. You were chosen for the role based on the full package you presented at the audition: your acting, your presence, and your look. If you change anything, it creates more work for the designers and the costume shop because they then have to adjust. If you lose ten pounds between being cast and show time, your measurements will be different, which means your clothing will have to be altered or repurchased. Of course, there are always exceptions to the rule. If you break a wrist or foot, adjustments will be made to accommodate you.

   I designed costumes for the play **"From the Mississippi Delta,"** *by Endesha Ida Mae Holland* and on the first show of the second weekend, one of the actors came in with a brand new hair weave that came all the way down to the middle of her back. Mind you, she was one of two young ladies who were playing a single character. On the first weekend, they both had beautiful Afros, so when she walked in with all that hair, I couldn't believe it! I didn't have time to say anything because as soon as the director walked in and saw it, she made her take it out before the performance began.

2. Performers, if you are in a period production, acrylic nails should not even be a question. I mean, really!

3. Performers, it is expected that you will maintain the hairstyle you auditioned with, unless you have had an explicit conversation with the designer and director.

4. In fittings, your job is to stand there and be an actor. Do not help with the fitting by pulling at the clothes, and definitely no commentary is necessary! We do not need your suggestions on

what you think you should wear instead. Do not bring your own clothes or shoes and we do not care if you like it or not. Just stand there, be pretty, and let us do our job!

5. Be sure to stand up straight when the hem is being pinned. If you are looking down during this process, the hem will be too short when you straighten up, forcing the costumer to re-pin it.

6. As long as your costume fits, is not restricting your movement, and isn't hurting you, you do not have to "like" it. The designer did not create the costume for *you*; they created it for your character. The only question in your head should be, "Does it feel good?" If a designer makes the mistake of asking you if you like the costume, politely answer, "Do you like it?" If they say yes, your response should be, "Then that's really all that matters." If they insist on you answering, tell them the truth, they asked for it!

7. "I would never wear this," is an inappropriate comment for a performer to make to a designer. They have read the script, conducted research, and collaborated with the director and other designers. Your comment sends the message that they don't know what they're doing. Here is a conversation I had with an actor:

   Actor - "I would never wear this."
   Me - "Would your character wear it?"
   Actor - "She would wear anything."

Me - "Then what's your point?"
Actor - "It just makes me look fat."
Me - "You're beautiful just the way you are."

(But you can imagine what I wanted to say.)

8. Performers, if you know you have a fitting, please wear the undergarments you will be wearing in the show, unless they are specialty garments, in which case they will be provided to you by the Costume Shop Supervisor.

9. **NEVER** come to a fitting and say the words, "I don't have any underwear on." For everyone's sake, **PLEASE DON'T!!**

10. Be sure you are hygienically ready for your fitting. The costume shop does not want to work on sweaty or smelly garments. If you don't have time to shower beforehand, disposable washcloths are available at a very reasonable price. You can grab them at most neighborhood grocery stores and pharmacies.

11. Please come to your fitting on time! Just know that if you are late, you will get in where you fit in, so have a seat and be patient. Otherwise, the costume shop will get behind with their other appointments, and I know you don't want that!

12. Once you have been fully costumed, please do not change or add anything after the show opens. That means you don't change your makeup, hair, jewelry, socks, NOTHING!! If something does need to be changed, you must get the permission of the designer.

13. Please hang up your costumes after each show; the crew does not perform maid duties.

14. DO NOT smoke or eat food of any kind while you are in your costume. And water is the only liquid you should consume while in costume. Not adhering to these rules creates stains and extra work for the costume crew. I always bring a robe that I can leave at the theatre, not only so that I can have a bite, but also to protect the garments when I'm touching up my makeup at intermission.

15. Please communicate any damage to a costume piece as soon as you are aware. Waiting to report it will only make the problems bigger as time goes on.

16. As with techies, if your hair is brightly colored, I strongly suggest you invest in a black skull cap or hoodie. The idea behind crew members being in all black is to make you as invisible as possible so that you do not distract from the atmosphere of the play.

17. Costume run crew, I suggest you make or purchase a short, black apron with many pockets for the run of the show. It will hold pins, small scissors, hair accessories, rubber bands, etc. in case of emergency. And make sure everything is secure so that when you bend down, nothing will fall off the apron making noise which would be a distraction during the show.

18. Designers, do not ask your actor if they "like" their costume. They are not there to approve of the design; they are there to ensure it fits and feels good. If they don't like it and don't want to hurt your feelings, you are forcing them to lie. If you like it and the director approves, that's all that matters.

19. Designers, be mindful of what needs to happen in the costume. Do they have to roll around on the floor? Are they doing splits? Does the costume get wet or dirty? Is fake blood a part of the costumes?

20. Directors! Have a clear vision of what you want in the world of the play!

    As a designer, I have worked with directors who simply say, "Oh, just make it pretty," or "just put them in some clothes." **I DON'T KNOW WHAT TO DO WITH THAT!** In almost all of those instances, I have had to design and redesign and re-shop a show because the director couldn't see the look until they saw the look. It was so frustrating and time-consuming that I have placed them on my "do not work with again" list.

21. Directors, if an actor comes to you complaining about their costume after we have agreed on the look, send them to the Stage Manager, Wardrobe Supervisor, or the Designer. DO NOT engage! Stay in your lane! You get in my costumes; I get in your directing!

22. On that same note, directors, please know whether you need a designer or a shopper or costume coordinator. *(Someone to get or order what you want)*. If you are going to design the show yourself, you don't need a designer. When you do that, you insult the integrity of the creative. You're sending a message that you know how to do this better than they do, even though they are trained and experienced.

    I was hired to design a show, and after meeting with the director, my gut told me that it was going to be a problem. I didn't listen and forged on, hoping it would get better. What she shared with me was completely against what the script called for. The show was set in a rural town where the people were excited about finally getting a Walmart. That's how rural the setting was. What the director showed me was characters that looked like they had stepped out of *GQ Magazine*. I tried as gently and as respectfully as I could to help her see that her vision was in contrast to what the story asked for. After much conversation, we came to a compromise and agreed on the look for the show. I shopped, had fittings, and changed whatever she asked me to. However, a week before opening, she had re-designed the entire show to look like her initial *GQ* vision without consulting with me at all. It was a complete waste of my time and energy. The producer apologized profusely and asked what they could do to make it up to me. I told her not to put my name in the program and never to call me again. I also informed her that I would not attend any of the performances. She understood and paid me in full.

23. Directors, please don't make your vision bigger than your budget! If you want a crystal ball gown for one of your actors, be sure you have crystal ball gown money!

24. Producers, Costume Designers and Hair/Makeup Artists are two different professions. Never assume a costume designer does makeup and hair and vice versa. Even if they are proficient in both, they require two different contracts! Stop it!!

25. Professional Costume Designers **DO NOT** do laundry or maintenance, so don't even ask! We design costumes, and our job is effectively done on opening night. Have the check ready!

Costuming is one of those thankless jobs that hardly ever gets any accolades. Therefore, be respectful and kind to everyone on the costume team: the run crew, stitchers, cutters, drapers, milliners, craftsmen, shop managers/supervisors, and designers, including hair and makeup creators. They can be your best dream or your worst nightmare. They hold the key to how you look on stage. Think about that.

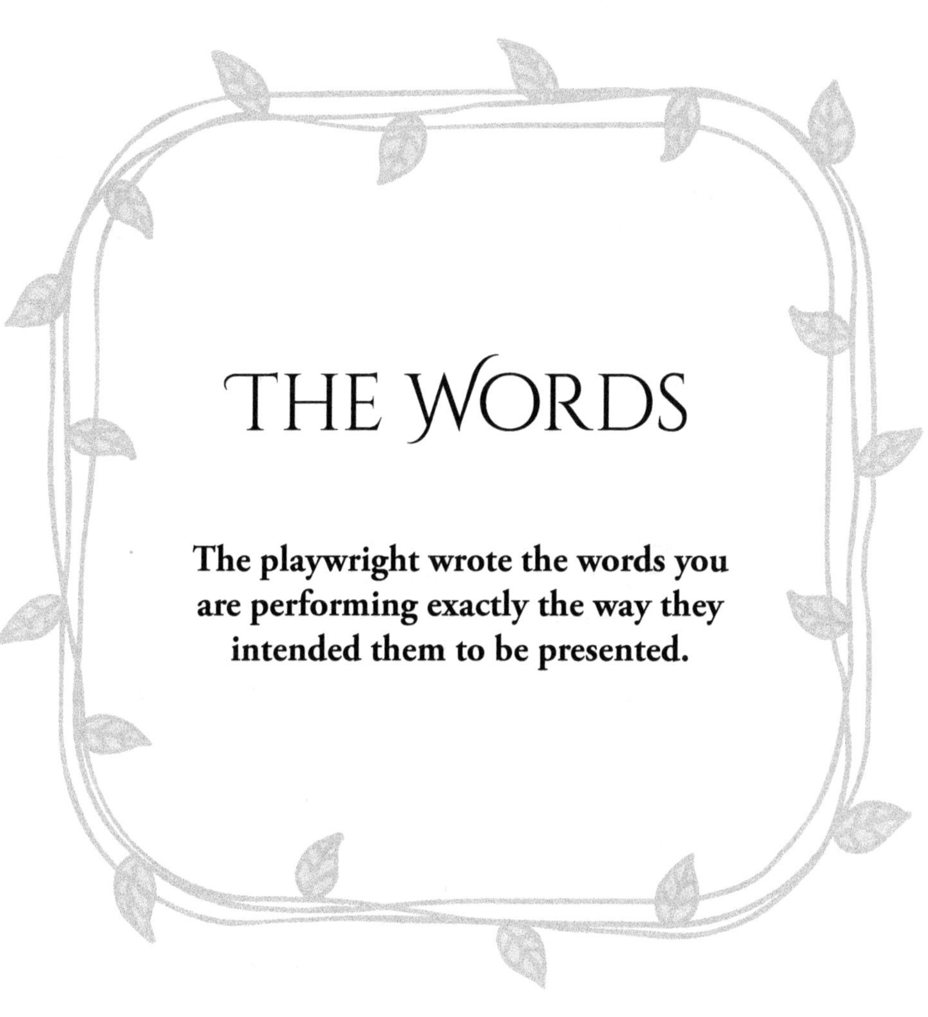

THE WORDS

The playwright wrote the words you are performing exactly the way they intended them to be presented.

When I was about to graduate from grad school, "Staying True to the Script" was my thesis topic. As an actress, it always bothered me when a director would change things the playwright specifically asked for because "I think this is better," without having done the research to find out why the writer chose that particular direction or those particular words. It also disturbed me as a writer because I felt like I was betraying the author.

One director that I worked with on numerous occasions had gained a reputation for "tinkering with scripts," as one reviewer pointed out. He'd take out entire paragraphs because he thought they were unnecessary, omit songs because his choice was better, or even change the wording and allow actors to ad-lib sentences if that's what they felt.

Another director changed the order of scenes so drastically that the author could not be invited to the performance for fear of the production being sued. One changed the song in a historical piece to a modern song and although it got lots of laughs, it fundamentally changed the dynamic of the story. Yet another director changed the ethnicity of the character I was playing. When the estate got wind of it, they threatened to shut down the show if the original casting was not reinstated! That forced me to have to sell the character, dressed in one culture while speaking the language of another. It was a challenging experience, but out of respect for the director, I believe I did it successfully.

In each of these instances, my job as an actor was to develop the character to the fullest according to the director's instructions. I left the politics to the producers and stayed as close to the script as I could. I also chose not to work as an actress with those directors again.

The Writer's Process

What it takes to write a script begins with the idea of a story. It may be one sentence or a few paragraphs of the overall narrative; it just depends on what the inspiration is. You may question whether the story is even relevant, but you know you've been called to tell it, so you have no choice but to write. Then you have to figure out who the players will be and how many of them there will be. What does the setting look like, what time period is it in, what time of day is it, or does the action span more than a day? These are just a few of the questions that arise before you even start the actual writing. Once you create the story line, you have to give voice to these people, making sure they don't all sound like you. That means you then have to research the who, what, when, where, and why of these characters and places. For instance, if they are in the rural south, you have to know what people sound like in that region, what their economic status was in that time period, and so on. Sometimes, it will come together immediately, and sometimes it may take years before it's completed. But once it is finished after numerous rewrites, the time comes to hear it out loud. This means setting up a table read with actors who have no idea how much blood, sweat and tears you've put into it but yet get to give their honest opinion about it. *(I can feel the anxiety right now as I'm writing this sentence).* Nonetheless, you sit down at the reading and listen to words being jumbled, skipped, mispronounced, and hear what you thought were powerful lines falling flat because either the actor didn't get it, or you weren't clear. You also hear how funny, enlightened, delightful, and profound some of the messages are, but you still realize they need to be tweaked a bit. When the reading is over, you brace yourself because now you get to hear everyone's opinion. You have to be brave enough to endure this because sometimes the comments are insensitive or miss the mark altogether and you have to explain and justify why you wrote what you wrote. You take all the notes, go home, and have to get yourself together because you're in your feelings, even though a lot of the criticism was correct. However, it feels like someone slapped your baby in the face and you had to stand there and watch without retaliating. You rewrite and rewrite and rewrite some more until you feel you've got a good product. Then you may enter it in staged reading festivals to get exposure and more feedback, only to discover that some of the directors in the audience think it needs to be workshopped. That means engaging in a collaborative process of revising, critiquing, and refining your work with a group of writers, actors, and/or other creative minds. At this juncture, you are insulted because you thought it was done, but now, you've got to go back to the writing table.

When I was at the stage reading for my play, **"Message from an Ancestor,"** the questions came immediately. Someone asked, "How would anyone even produce this with part of the setting being on a seashore in Africa? And do you know how strong an actress would have to be to pull this off?" I hadn't thought about that because my focus was on the story. So, I had to rewrite some more. Once I was satisfied with it, it was accepted into several festivals as a staged reading. When I saw what the directors and actors did with it, I knew what I needed to do to finish it, and I did.

Once you have finished the play, it's time to shop it around to see who might be interested in producing it. Sometimes it'll get produced quickly, sometimes it'll take a while, and sometimes you just keep waiting. When someone does decide to produce it, you have to contend with who the director is and who they cast, which you have no input on. That's where anxiety again rears its ugly head, because you have no idea what you'll see on opening night. Most of the time, you will not be a part of the rehearsal process.

There you are, sitting in your reserved seat. The lights go down, the announcement is made explaining the rules of the theatre, and then the lights come up. What you are looking at may or may not be what you envisioned, but there you are. No matter what, you have to accept what was presented with grace and be thankful that your play was given life.

The point is that there is an insurmountable amount of time, energy, and creativity invested in writing these stories. Staying true to the script, exactly as it was written, is showing respect to the playwright who painstakingly wrote every word. If you ad-lib two or more words or add a whole sentence, you are rewriting the script, and who are you to do that? The message you are sending the playwright is that you know how to write their story better than they did. Really?! Well here's a newsflash for you: If you think the line would sound better the way you think it should read, put it in your own script! If you pay attention, you will notice that scripts have a rhythm; it's up to you to find it. As an actor, that is part of the job!

Audience Member

When you are an audience member, show the same respect you would want if you were on stage.

When you go to the theatre, please be mindful of the fact that everyone who bought a ticket is coming to spend time in an alternate universe for a few hours. They intentionally come to hear someone else's story from beginning to end without interruption. They want to imagine themselves in that world or feel emotions for the characters and their situations. They came to laugh, cry, gasp, be in awe, be in horror, connect, root for the underdog, understand the journey or perhaps support the actors. That experience begins in the lobby when you are looking at the actor headshots, examining the poster about the show, or perhaps viewing the exhibit that offers a glimpse into what is to come. When the lights in the lobby flicker three times, that is not the time to go to the restroom. That's a clear indication that the show is about to begin.

It's Show Time!

1. When the lights go down, put your phone on silent and put it away. Please, the magical world of theatre is about to begin!

2. Please refrain from talking during the performance. You can discuss how you feel after you have left the building.

3. If you don't open that candy before the show starts, you should be arrested! That cellophane paper, for some reason, amplifies in the theatre and disturbs EVERYBODY! It rips the audience out of the world of the play and places their focus entirely on when you're finally going to get it open!!

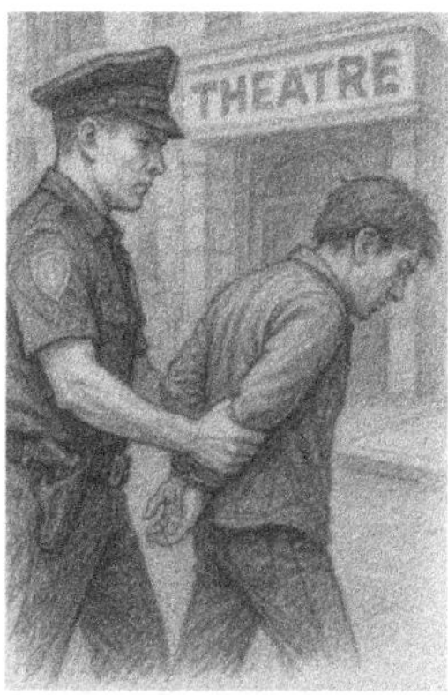

4. Texting during the show disturbs the people on either side of you and behind you. Hiding it in your lap or behind your program does not work; the light from the screen is distracting. Put it away!

5. When the announcer says, "there will be no videotaping or photography allowed," that means you! **PUT YOUR PHONE ON SILENT AND PUT IT AWAY!**

6. When your phone goes off during the performance, it takes EVERYONE out of the world of the play because now everyone is focused on your phone! To avoid this at all costs, turn the phone off or put it on airplane mode! But if, by some chance, it does go off, make sure you can get to it as quickly as possible. Having to hear it continuously ring while you dig around the bottom of your purse or try to get it out of your pocket is nerve-racking! And for heaven's sake, please don't answer it!

   I was in the audience at a performance and heard someone's phone ring. Not only did they answer the phone, but they also got up and began a whole conversation while walking across the front of the stage. Did they leave the theatre? NO! They went to the back of the auditorium, thinking they were whispering and when they finished the conversation, walked back across the front of the stage, and took their seat. Were they finished? NO! The phone rang a second time, and they repeated their actions! I was mortified! Not only for the other audience members, but the poor actors were visibly disturbed as they tried to stay in character and continue the story. These were professional actors, and even though they persevered, I could see even they were thrown off.

7. If you are late for any performance, understand that you are already a disruption because you are pulling focus from the stage and onto you. Please try to be as quiet as you possibly can. Don't make it worse by having a conversation with the usher because you want to find the exact seat on your ticket.

8. If you come to the show late, please sit in the seats closest to the door or in the back no matter what your ticket says. The show has started and the people who were on time are already engrossed in the story. You take them out of it when they have to get up, wait for you to cross over them, help you not fall because it's dark and do all they can to avoid vocally engaging with you. Slide in, sit down quickly and hush!

9. If you are inebriated when you are going to a live performance, please consider staying home. You have no sense of how loud you are, no control over your responses and almost always have to use the restroom before intermission. Spare us!

Look at it this way. Go to the theatre ready to immerse yourself in another world without being a distraction to that world in any way. That's what everyone paid to be a part of.

EXTRA ADVICE

Because I want you to succeed

- You have chosen a hard profession. Therefore, you will need a strong support system. First, get a job that will pay your bills while you are in pursuit of your dream. Hopefully, you can find something that will allow you to audition during the day for film and/or in the evenings for theatre.

- Understand that there are many actors waiting for the opportunity to do what you do. The key is to be committed and consistent. If this is what you want, don't ever give up!

- You should always be looking for the next gig. After you have been cast in one show, start looking for what's next.

- Update your headshot and resume regularly. If you make any drastic changes to your appearance, change your headshot! When you show up for the audition, the casting agent and/or director want to see the same person "in the photograph" standing in front of them.

- To live the life of an artist, you have to love it! Loving it means putting in the work, which requires it to be on your mind all the time.

- When you're "constantly" ready, you never have to "get" ready.

- When you hear a monologue from someone else and you love it, "steal" it. No one owns it *(unless they wrote it)*. Just remember it's not that you can do it better, it's that you can do it differently.

- Know that it is never too late to be what you would have or should've been. Even if you have to take a break from the craft to handle whatever life throws at you, keep studying, reading, and learning.

- Broadway is in you, so practice excellence no matter where you are. You don't have to be in California or New York to be a success. Enjoy being a big fish in a little pond if that works better for you.

- When you get that big break, be smart about it, because the business is fickle. You may ride high for a while and then it may take a long time before your next break comes. Before you go buying expensive cars and large houses that you may or may not be able to maintain, buy yourself a modest little house somewhere that you love so that no matter what happens, you will always have a place to live.

- Once you make it, get yourself an accountant and don't let any checks go out without your knowledge. Keep a close eye on your funds at all times. We've heard the stories of celebrities losing everything because they trusted somebody else with their money. If you don't know how to handle it all, take some business classes so you know how to protect yourself financially.

We are walking, talking, art pieces that were created by the Creator who chose you to represent their work. Make them proud.

Ms. Margarette

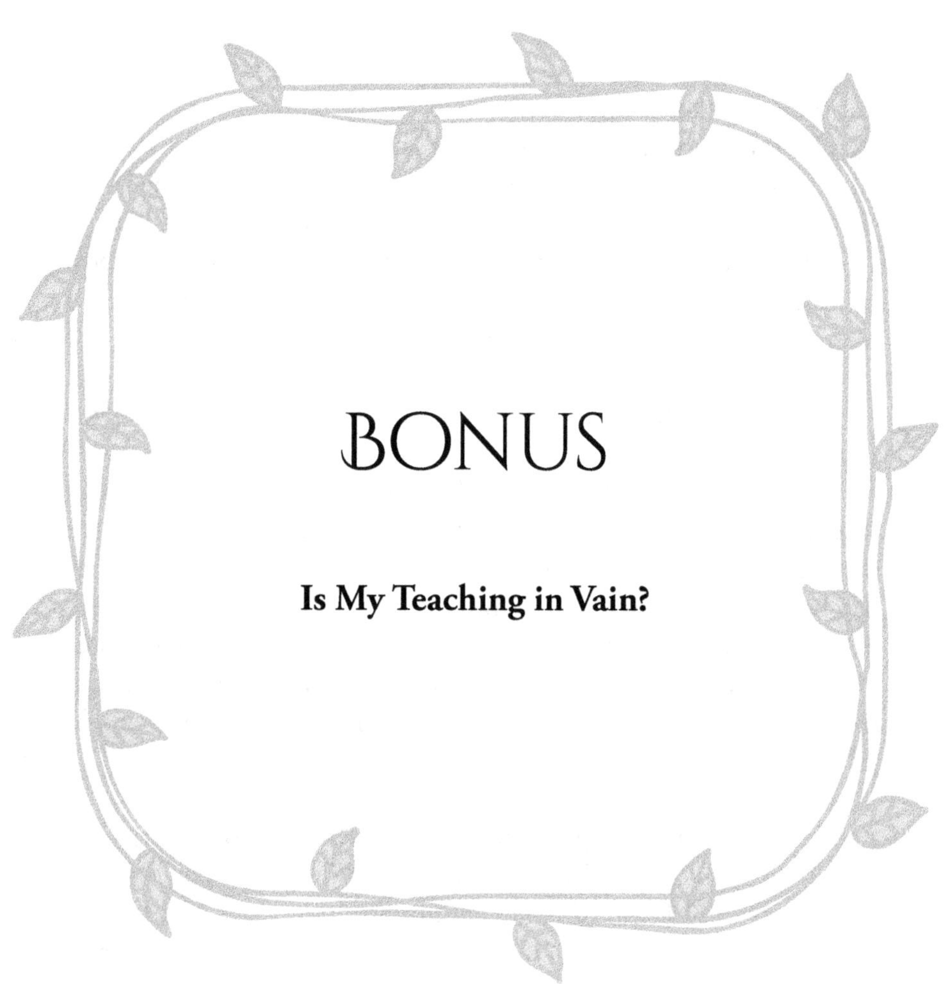

BONUS

Is My Teaching in Vain?

I sat in full regalia at the graduation ceremony of my jubilant students who were graduating from the theatre program I'd acquired. I smiled back at excited faces using the "Alba Emoting" tool I'd learned in graduate school from Janet Rogers, to ensure they didn't see that my heart was weeping for them.

I had given them everything I could, including love, as the only full-time Assistant Professor in the program. I thought about how grateful they had been to be a part of an actual production, as most of them had never experienced it. I recalled how overwhelmed they were when they realized what it took to produce a theatrical show. I thought about how proud they were when they took their first bow in front of a live audience and the genuine hugs and gratitude I'd received afterward for giving them something to be proud of.

I thought about how heavy my heart became when juniors in the program had no idea what actor's blocks *(the wooden cubes used for furniture during rehearsal)* were. I had built them for their training soon after my arrival. I thought about the first time I talked with them and discovered that they didn't know the basics of theatre. They had been taking classes with no instructor, paid for those classes, and obviously learned nothing in them. As an adjunct, I would get some of them together outside of class to teach them what I knew about the subjects they were supposed to be learning with the then one full-time instructor.

As I sat there reminiscing on their accomplishments, other thoughts crossed my mind: "Am I teaching in vain? What more could I have done for them?" Then I thought about how many times I had talked with administration, trying to get them to understand the program and why they needed to support it. I thought about all the reports I'd put together to illustrate how far the program had to grow just to become average. I visualized the blank faces staring back at me as I pleaded for them to at least fix the building so that their students wouldn't have to smell the stench of stagnant water, where the rain had seeped in through the broken windows so much that the walls were buckling. I recalled how I'd rallied my friends from the artistic community to come and help me to help them and the fact that they came simply because I called and then were dismissed without so much as a thank you from anyone but me.

I thought about the opportunities they'd gotten because of my ties to the community and countless hours I'd spent teaching six to eleven classes per semester, while directing shows I'd somehow managed to produce with my own money. I recalled how I had stayed up late into the night making costumes, designing sets, and working on layouts for the flyers and the program. I remembered doing all this on a salary that was less than what a high school drama teacher would make. The issues with the program far outweighed any more giving I could've possibly mustered.

I listened intently to speaker after speaker go on and on about the students' bright futures and how they were now prepared to take on the world and make them all proud. I looked at my students beaming with joy as their name was called. I saw them jumping up and down and even giving praise shouts as they crossed the stage. Tears welled in my eyes as I smiled and waved to them, not only because they had reached the goal of receiving their diploma, but also because I knew they were not fully prepared to go on the professional journey that lay ahead. As hard as I tried, the tears that had been tucked away safely in my heart escaped.

I hoped that they would be the ones that could break through the inevitable and not end up like their predecessors, who now worked at restaurants, daycare centers, and retail stores. These are all noble professions, but not what they paid four years of college for. I prayed they would not become like their classmate valedictorian who, three years after graduating with a Bachelor of Fine Arts, still worked in a bowling alley. I prayed that somehow, some way, they'd be able to get into a graduate school somewhere, but in my heart, I knew. I knew, I prayed, and I wept.

So, the question is, am I teaching in vain? The answer is no. Some students understand the value of what I passed on to them, even though it was hard. They have taken what I've taught them and gone on to have successful careers on Broadway and in film. It has, I must admit, gotten harder to convey clearly what this profession has done for so many of us who grew up in a theatre space that commanded respect. The hunger that was instilled in us to give a performance everything we had, not for ourselves, but for the audience and our director. We valued the fact that someone paid to see us tell these important stories. We understood that when we were on stage, we could be heard without interruption. We relished the idea of being in a whole different world than the one we lived in and, for just a few hours, we could become someone else! I look forward to the day that I walk into a theatre space and see actors warming up, going over their lines, walking the stage, checking props, and immersing themselves in the world of the play without a phone in their hand. Will that ever happen? I don't know. But with this book, I will rest assured that I did all I could to make it so.

SPECIAL THANKS

Earlie K. Joyner for always having my back!
&
Emily Claudette Freeman, The best coach EVER!
Hali Hutchison-Houk, Consultant
Jeremy Morris, Contributor

About the Author

Margarette Joyner, a retired educator, holds degrees from the University of South Alabama, Mobile *(BFA)* and Virginia Commonwealth University *(MFA)*. After graduating, she answered the call and taught at several universities for more than a decade. She is a dynamic and powerful actress, director, playwright, and award-winning costume designer. Her collection of historical garments entitled, **"A Legacy of Elegance,"** has been exhibited across the country. She also has publications which include **"Message From an Ancestor,"** and **"When I Kill Him, Jesus Can Have Him."**

NOTES

www.ingramcontent.com/pod-product-compliance
Lightning Source LLC
LaVergne TN
LVHW010942110826
845149LV00013B/2717

* 9 7 9 8 9 9 3 8 0 8 9 2 5 *